HUMAN APOLOGY

Author

GOPIKA UNNI. P

SHANLAX PUBLICATIONS
SHANLAX #SINCE1990

HUMAN APOLOGY

First Edition: 2020

ISBN: 978-93-90082-16-2

Price: Rs.235/-

Publisher

SHANLAX PUBLICATIONS
61, 66 T.P.K. Main Road
Vasantha Nagar
Madurai – 625003
Tamil Nadu, India

Ph: 0452-4208765,
Mobile: 7639303383
email:publisher@shanlaxpublications.com
web: www.shanlaxpublications.com

A NOTE TO HUMANS

HUMANS ! THE ONLY SPECIES WHO DIG THEIR OWN GRAVES.

IT'S NEVER TOO LATE TO APOLOGIZE FOR YOUR CALLOUS SELF-CENTRED DEEDS.

THERE'S STILL A CHANCE TO TURN THE GRAVES TO GARDENS.

FOREWORD

Gopika Unni's poems resonate with an uncanny acumen to sieve through any form of inequity around us- be that of gender, color-ism or identity. These politicized collages are the responses of a sensitive mind treading through the rough labyrinth of life while simultaneously preserving a child-like innocence. Though this is her debut collection of poetry; she is shorn of confessional rendering that otherwise permeate Indian English Poetry.

Genuine concerns of the feminine psyche questioning gender stereotypes testify to the time tested dictum that a woman with a pen is lethal. My best wishes to this talented poet.

S. CHANDRAMOHAN
POET

CONTENTS

THE DEVILISH GAZE

A verse for the entire women world
A verse on their cordial experience.

Hazy perspectives glide
In our barren mind.

Those eyes which stare on our breasts.
Those eyes which gaze foxily on our lips.

'The' ogle spotted
In the hullabaloo.

'The' gaze perceived
In the hustle of buses, trains.

'The' gape and 'The' awk
From the male eyes.

A tinge of disgust pop up

A shade of tears crop up

From the weary women.

The so called victims of

Laura Mulvey's 'MALE GAZE.'

THE RUSTED FEATHERS

Watching the sky moving away
Through the bars.

She dreamed of flying high
In the unbounded sky.

She longed of touching the stars
She desired for the hug of air;
And the touch of crimson rays.

The caged bird perched
On the rails;
Singing for her Utmost freedom.

Confined within the bars
Of patriarchal norms;
Exiguous of her words.

The caged bird perched
On the rails;
Singing for her
Utmost freedom.

Trapped in the prejudice
Of casteism
Biased by the plague
Of racism.

The caged bird perched
On the rails;
Singing for her utmost freedom.

Cramped in the terms
And norms of quarantine.
Scared of a tiny virus.

The caged bird perched
On the rails;
Singing for her utmost freedom.

The caged bird sings, longs and croons...
Her wings will never fade out;
Even if she is immured
In a dark cage.

THE OMNIPRESENT VIRUS

Inhaled by a speck of dust.
Intoxicated by the drug;
Of Casteism.

Some gets addicted
Some gets frenzied
Some tags their identity
In the label of caste.

Caste, the Omnipresent Virus
Sucks away the nectar
Of happiness;
Of harmony;
Of love.

Castiest era prevails
The digital era.

GREEN ARMY

Covetous tides of mankind
Seared the crust of earth.

The blood sucking smile
Of progress
Swallows the denizens
Of doomed wild life.

Man's desirous, ceaseless
Thirst for money.
And the earth makes
A pompous parade of disaster.

DIGITAL FIRE

Glance at the world
You see infront.

Advance after advance;
Our needs and commands
In our finger tips.

Enhance after enhance;
The choices we make
In the web sources.

The world stares
On the gleamy screen.

The window of information
At our fingertips.

Books lost its smell;
Grass unfurled;
On the playgrounds.

The Digital Fire spreads.
Glued to the technology;
Crounched over computers
And mobile phones.

Eye to eye conversation
Fades away.
Eyes of technological robots
Haunt us.

The Digital world
Chained man,
Where he fails
To escape.

THE AGONY

Hard labour in
Torrid days.
Beating sweaty days of
Scorching sun;
Dreaming for their harvest.

Agony and pain
Filled in their eyes.

Brooding over
Their unpredictable future.

They toil the soil;
Anticipates for positivity of harvest

But fate showers them;
The cloud of despair.
Child's haunting eyes;
Wife's pathetic smile.

Hurt is too much
To bear.
Pain is too much
To wear.

Trapped in the web of debts.
The powerless farmers.
The ultimate losers.
Falls into the hands of suicide.

THE BARDS OF RESISTANCE

By slashing the dark blind
Shield of Untouchability.

By traversing through
The foul pit of castiesm.

By rising from the call
Of an untouchable scape goat
By the Varna system.

They shined;
The Dalit poets;
The Bards of Resistance.

The Dalit activists;
The followers of the firebrand
Revolutionary leader, B.R. Ambedkar.

They sing the songs of
Equality, Fraternity and Brotherhood.

DEVOURING LUST

The fire of lust
Like a pesticide poisoning
the whole body
lits the Sin of rape.

A world of sexuality
Crepts in
Degrading the world of morality.

Rape happens within
Days, weeks, months, years
like the global climatic changes.

The most frequently
happening Sin.

Rapists growl at the law
with a flicker
in their monstrous eyes.

Newspapers, social media, magazines
celebrate the rape
enititled with emotional headlines
and hashtags.

But the ultimate loser
is the victim,
The Woman.

Without the baggage of love;
And kindness
Without care and respect;
This fire of lust keeps burning.

CARNAGE

Man becomes deaf
By greed and by choice.

Have a glimpse of look
on to the future earth.

A lifeless world;
An empty core;
A barren land;
Like T.S. Eliot's "Waste Land"
Of Nothingness.

GUEST LABOURERS

A glittering ray of hope
Enshrined in their hearts.

Miles and miles to migrate.
Yet, they migrate
Like the migratory birds
And fishes
To a new land
Of aspirations;
Departing from
Their own mother land.

The migrant workers
Bearing a tag
Of otherised identity.

Civilized folks yelled at them:
"THE OTHERS", "THE MIGRANTS", "THE GUEST LABOURERS."

Falling out of the box
Of general.

The back breakers.
The sedulous beings;
Slogging without
Any encouragement.
Calling them as
The cheapest labourers,
But making use of their
Each and every sweat drops.

A repugnance to sit
Along with them.

A revulsion to dine

With them.

Why this so called "otherising"

And "aversion" towards the guest labourers?

THE MASKED CULTURE

Man is born free
But now everywhere he is being locked up.

The genesis of a new era;
With masks and santizers
As the inevitable products for wholly.

The desolate world devoid
Of all transportation.

No trace of human life
Anywhere.

As there is an unseen mighty
Monster outside:
Wearing the mask of death.

Man now welcomes

The neighbours

With a smile of suspicion in their eyes.

Social distancing averts

Us from multitude

Of parties and gatherings.

"Be cautious to venture out."

The mind alerted.

The virus of fear

Chains the man

Enduring thoughts of demise.

It is not Ben Jonson's

"The Masque Of Blackness"

But The Mask of Quarantine;

Living an indoor life

With the fear of

A microscopic particle.

Where stands your power and wealth now?

As Shakespeare says:

"Seeking the bubble reputation

Is pointless."

The Quarantine of self recognition.

And the whole world

Is in a marathon

To save their lives.

OUTCRY OF NATURE

Darkness engulfed all the laughter.
Ceaseless rain deluged the nature.

Man's dreams, materialistic happiness....
All washed away with his tears.

Monsoons freezed the human life;
Swayed by heavy winds.

Weeping river caused the destruction
Devouring the nature
In an enormous rage.

The flood of misery.
The flood of doom.

The tide roars higher and higher...

Gloomy days of starvation.

Wiping off the metro cities

By mighty rivers.

All the eyes stare upon the sky

for the sunshine's rays.

The moan of aching hearts.

Nature, the creator proves

To be the master of man once again.

ROARING TIDES

He conquers everyone
With his invisible mighty hands.

He roars like
The tides of a sea.

He is more terrible
Than the terrorists.

He is more fearer
Than the cannon.

He has no caste
No race, no nativity

He has no discrimination
For haves and have not.

Hunger, the ultimate conqueror
Of humankind.

SOARING SOUL

Robert Burns, the Bard of Ayrshire
Sings:
"My love is like a red red rose."

Contemporary love is like a
"Revenge by acid attack."

She, the true warrior
Pens her memoirs
On Acid Attack.

That unexpected monster
Left her a lifetime scar.

The scar of deformation.
The scar of disfigured beauty.

She is neither a victim;
Nor a survivor;
Instead, she is the Phoenix,
Who rises from the charred remains.

She could burn him down to earth
With her mighty fire;
Instead she choose the fire to purify her.

The society stabs her
With unfavourable words
Showering displeasing remarks.

She articulates the grievesome
Monologue
With the lonesome moon.

She hides her face with a veil.
Mirror is her greatest foe;
The reflection of her impalpable face.

She is an epitome of will power
Who glows like an emerald.

She is the crimson red rose.
The frail creature gnaws away
Her petals;
With the touch of acid rain.
But her thorns are her pillars.

All he saw in her was her face;
But what he doesn't know was that
SHE is not just a fair outer skin.
And SHE rised.

RELICS OF CUSTOMS

Vivaah, Kanyadhaan, Swayamvaram...
The diversification continues
above the weight of
irreversible customs.

Marriage; Wedding;
The contemporary coinages.
The unity of two individuals.
The wedlock of patriarchy,
The male weds the female.

The million glued customs;
Women leave their houses,
Under the weight of
Wedding band.

The serpant of patriarchy
Spits the venom
On women.

Patriarchal marriage customs
As social constructs violates
The tag of equality.

The Queer marriages
Host the flag of equality,
Which bids farewell to gender dominancy.

THE AGE OF RENAISSANCE

Time to question the distinction
Of toys between between girls and boys.

Why the colour of "pink" for girls
And the colour of "blue" to boys?

The deep rooted gender inequality
in colours and toys.

Time to change the use of
Inscribed attributes
For girls and boys.

Why the adjective "disciplined"
And "well natured" falls before girls
And the "brave, "valiant"
Precedes the boys?

Time to raise voice against
The use of calling one
By castiest names.

Why the terms of
"Dalit, Pulaya, ezhava, Nair, Namboodiri"
Uttered?

Call one by their names
Not by their caste.

Time to unfollow the disdain
Towards the migratory workers.

Why they are being regarded
As the "otherized" from
The main sphere?

Treat all with the same dignity.
The Age of Renaissance parades.

Articulate the voice of resistance
To paint the portrait of "ONENESS".

• • •

THE BLISS

Unfold the note of darkness
Concealing your inner self

Let your eyes twinkle
Upon the lucid sky.
Shimmering joy.

Look on the hazy sunshine
With a tearful smile.

Let your ambiguous thoughts
To fly away in dusty wind.

Nature vibes are eternal;
Showers all around you
The bliss of happiness.

THE QUARANTINED SECOND CHILDHOOD

Looking into the
Shakespeare's seventh stage
Of life,
The second childhood.

A figure of stooped posture;
Wrinkled and brittle;
Shadowy fingers shaking
Constantly;

Withered lips murmer
The lyrics of religious texts.

We see a shadow of sadness
For their dependence on others.

A thought of loneliness
Crawled on them.

The home quarantined people
Of old age;
Devoid of any technological connectivity.

An embodiment of innumerable experiences;
Who engraved an inscription
In this stage of world.

Let us care them
Like a child;
Who once raised us
During our infancy.

THE SHADOW OF BEAUTY

Mirror reflects her
Mein as 'Dark.'

Her relatives enounce.
Her friends utter
The equivalent monologue
"You're Dark."

Advertisments render
The world of fairness.

Each castigates.
East lambastes.
The beauty of
Dark skinned girls.

Why the fair skinned girls be preferred
In the advertisements?

Why the fair skinned girls limned
In the brochure of beauty parlours?

Does fair skin only possess beauty?
Why our girls stick to these whitening creams?

Why the adjective 'fair' is mentioned
For girls in matrimony?

Why white is termed as the
Most attractive colour for feminine beauty?

How many dark skinned models
Appear in the cover pages of magazines?

Those questions exhibits
The sociological images.

Don't hide your race

In this fair world.

Let your Dark skin shines eternally

In this fair skinned world.

BLACK – THE RAPE VICTIM OF COLOURFUL WORLD

In the world of colours
Each one with specific beauty
For the viewer's eyes.

Colours with unique personalities
With unique labels...

Hundreds of unique good labels...
There stood a lonely figure
In this colour of magical world
-"**BLACK**" ;

The devilish colour of human concept
The colour of ultimate end "Death"

Colour of unhappiness.

Colour of mourning.

Thousands of inadorable labels for Black;

No place for black in VIBGYOR.

The colour which is being raped by all.

A plain rape victim of this

Colourful world...

POETRY

Poet's scribbled words of life;
With the wisdom of an owl.

Poetry is the poet to paper
Communication;
With the mediator of a pen
Mightier than the sword.

Poetry is a mode of expression;
An act of reaction;
An act of resistance;
Voice of voiceless
Through witty verses.

Overcomed by the myriad
Of emotions of protest, anger, dejection:
The birth of poetry transpired.

"LET'S JOIN OUR HANDS FOR A NOBLE CAUSE"

www.ingramcontent.com/pod-product-compliance
Lightning Source LLC
Chambersburg PA
CBHW050026170726
48282CB00025B/565
9789390082162